Parts of a Tree

Written by Katherine Chu

GRL Consultant, Diane Craig, Certified Literacy Specialist

Lerner Publications ◆ Minneapolis

Note from a GRL Consultant
This Pull Ahead leveled book has been carefully designed for beginning readers. A team of guided reading literacy experts has reviewed and leveled the book to ensure readers pull ahead and experience success.

Lerner Publications
An imprint of Lerner Publishing Group, Inc.
241 First Avenue North
Minneapolis, MN 55401 USA

For reading levels and more information, look up this title at www.lernerbooks.com.

Main body text set in Memphis Pro 24/39
Typeface provided by Linotype.

Photo Acknowledgments
The images in this book are used with the permission of: © Inga Nielsen/Shutterstock Images, p. 3; © Radovan1/Shutterstock Images, pp. 4–5; © Mohammad Hamid/Adobe Stock, pp. 6–7; © Montri Thipsorn/Shutterstock Images, pp. 8–9, 16 (right); © Nitr/Shutterstock Images, pp. 10–11, 16 (middle); © Jules_Kitano/Shutterstock Images, pp. 12–13, 16 (left); © Олег Кошевський/Adobe Stock, pp. 14–15.

Front cover: © Mikael Damkier/Adobe Stock

Library of Congress Cataloging-in-Publication Data

Names: Chu, Katherine, author.
Title: Parts of a tree / written by Katherine Chu.
Description: Minneapolis : Lerner Publications, [2025] | Series: In the garden (pull ahead readers - nonfiction) | Includes index. | Audience: Ages 4–7 | Audience: Grades K–1 | Summary: "Trees have many parts from the bottom all the way to the top! This simple, engaging text allows emergent readers to discover the parts of an apple tree. Pairs with the fiction title Grandpa's Trees"— Provided by publisher.
Identifiers: LCCN 2024009129 (print) | LCCN 2024009130 (ebook) | ISBN 9798765647790 (lib. bdg.) | ISBN 9798765661987 (pbk) | ISBN 9798765655597 (epub)
Subjects: LCSH: Trees—Juvenile literature. | Trees—Anatomy—Juvenile literature.
Classification: LCC QK475.8 .C468 2025 (print) | LCC QK475.8 (ebook) | DDC 582.16—dc23/eng/20240417

LC record available at https://lccn.loc.gov/2024009129
LC ebook record available at https://lccn.loc.gov/2024009130

Manufactured in the United States of America
1 – CG – 12/15/24

Table of Contents

Parts of a Tree

The tree has roots.

The tree has branches.

The tree has leaves.

The tree has flowers.

The tree has apples.

We like apple trees!

Did You See It?

apples

flowers

leaves

Index